praise for The Art of waking up

Brenda Taulbee's poems give my spine reverb, like poetry is meant to, like only poetry that matters, can.

> – Lidia Yuknavitch, *author, Verge, Book of Joan, Chronology of Water* and *The Small Backs of Children*

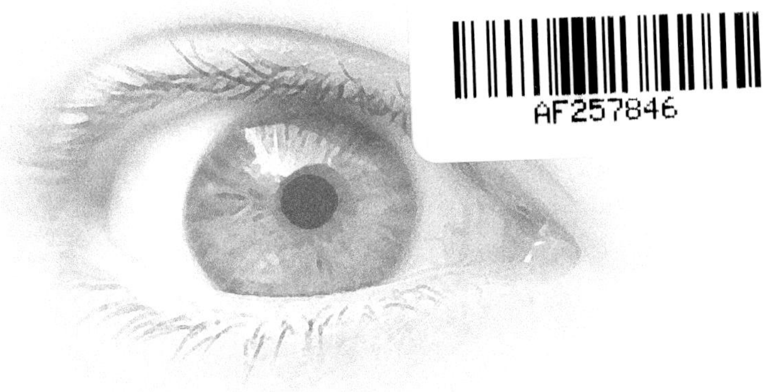

Brenda Taulbee's voice is a shriek parading as a whisper. Her poems are told like a secret, filled with yearning; both ephemeral and visceral at the same time.

> – Amy Temple Harper, *author, Cramped Uptown*

Brenda Taulbee's writing, beautiful and raw, brings readers with her to stand in the kitchen with her mother or describe the sounds of bones and body shifting and bending. Her stories keep you seeking more.

— *Nastashia Minto*, author, *Naked*

> Taulbee is a full force wind, a mountain, a river, a whisper, an echo, a flood, a tether, a lifeboat, a maker of new things, creator of beautiful worlds in the painful spaces in cruel realities.
>
> – Jenny Forrester, author, *Narrow River, Wide Sky* and *Soft-Hearted Stories*

Brenda Taulbee produces clouds of circumstantial items recognizable to most of us who have lives: a mattress strapped to a jeep, the kindness of a stranger in a heavy rain storm, that little tab broken off the back of the video control.

– Douglas Spangle, author, *A White Concrete Day: Poems: 1978 – 2013*, recipient, Stewart H. Holbrook Literary Legacy Award

Brenda Taulbee **is** a mushroom not in my field guide. Her poetry is graffiti composed as an exquisite tattoo. I stare at inscriptions carved into her flesh while trying to avoid eye contact.

> – *Casey Bush*, author, *Student of the Hippocampus*,
> editor, *Bear Deluxe*

Brenda Taulbee knows that these narrative kits, often tricky, with traps of self-justification, self-delusion, are also life rafts.

> – *R. V. Branham*, author, *A New Order of the Phylum, Curse & Berate in 69+ Languages*, ed., *Gobshite Quarterly*

PIRMÂ DIENA. RIGA LATVIJA PREMIER JOUR
08.02.92
ALBERTVILLE '92

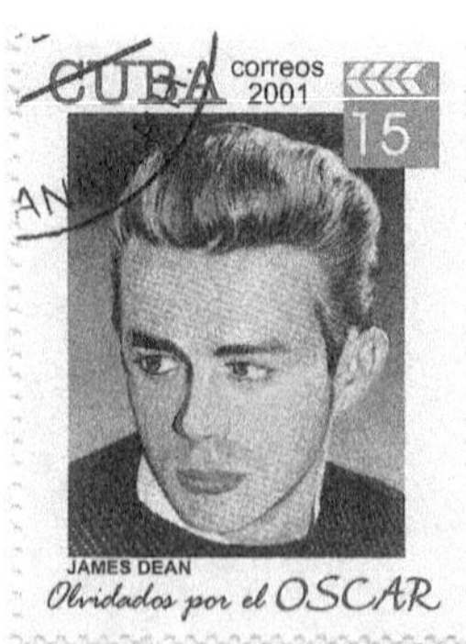

CUBA correos
2001
15
JAMES DEAN
Olvidados por el OSCAR

The Art of Waking Up:

62 Poems & A Song of Despair: 2012 – 2015 *

Brenda Taulbee

Reprobate/GobQ Books
Portland, Oregon

*) 2nd. edition, rev., incl. recent poems, May, 2020

THIS IS A REPROBATE BOOK PUBLISHED BY GOBQ BOOKS

IISBN 978-1684544691 \// $15.00

Digital Edition Pending, honest ...

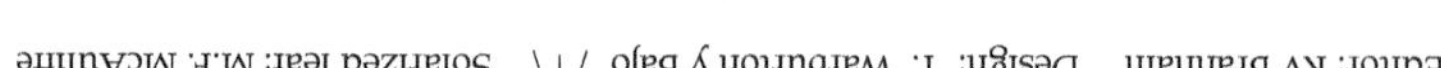

Editor: RV Branham   Design: T. Warburton y Bajo /|/ Solarized leaf: M.F. McAuliffe

Curry Love Dance (Baby Baby Baby) orig. in *The Art of Being Human, vol. 9* (ed., Daniela Voicu); *Wish You Were Here* orig. appeared in *Keep It Weird*, a Poetry Box publication; *Inchworm Lullaby* orig. in *Decades Review*, Is. 11, 2014; *I Am A Known Breaker of Broken Things, When Making Lemonade, Razorblades & India Ink, & The Night Our Friendship Fell Down The Stairs* have been in *Gobshite Quarterly* (2013, 2014, 2015); many of the other pces appeared in the chapbook *Dances With Bears*, with different titles. (& some have been revised.) *When I Asked You To, How to Choose the Perfect Avocado, On that Couch in the Yard at the Edge of Adulthood, You Cast Yourself into the Desert Where There is No Air, Geode Heart/Break* appeared in *Gobshite Quarterly* betw. 2016 & 2018. All titles appearing in *Gobshite Quarterly* were published *en face* & tr. into several languages.

The 1st. ed. was made possible, in part by a matching grant from Micro Enterprise Services of Oregon, in part by freshly juiced smoothies, & in very large part by all-nighters, & pots & pots of freshly ground French/Med. Roast; the 2nd. ed. has been co-sponsored by kombucha, & by freshly-ground & cold brew coffee.

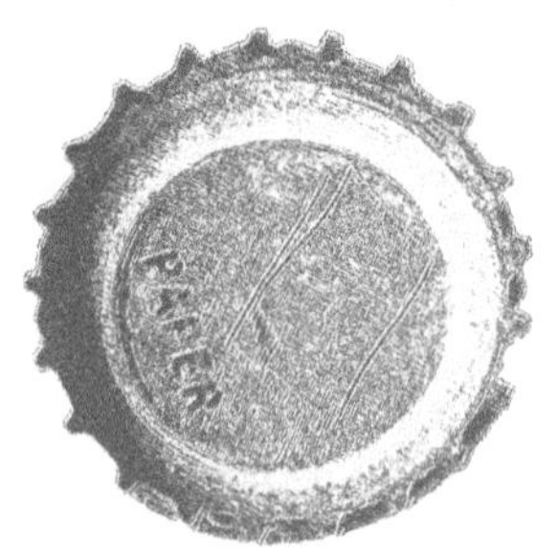
PAPER

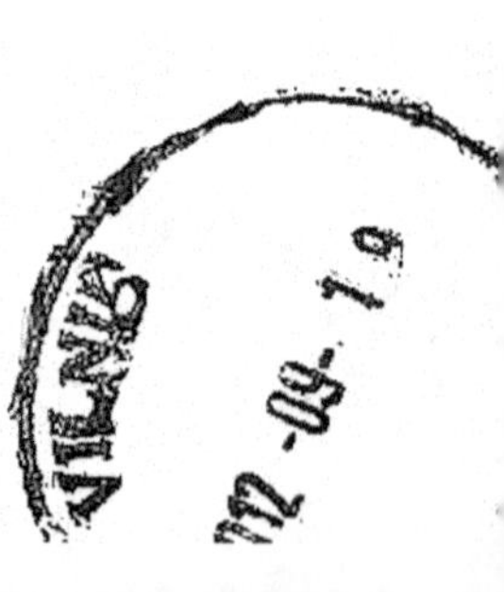
VILNIUS
'12 -09- 10

CONTENTS

Poverty	13
Because My Father Was A Mtn.	14
After Each War	15
Inchworm Lullaby	16
Whether You Remove A Bandaid	18
The Art of Waking Up	18
I Am A Known Breaker of Broken Things	20
6-Word Stories (i.)	22
The Night our Friendship Fell Down The Stairs	22
Down By the Bay Where Lighthouses	24
Meet Me, Let Me	25
Today at the Bus Stop	25
6-Word Stories (ii.)	26
Year of the Bear	26
Razor Blades & India Ink	29
Futsal is Not Rugby	29
All Your Faces Look the Same	30
On Missing: Part i.	32
Let's Set Out Before the Sun Comes Up...	33
When You Make Lemonade	34
582 Miles	35
Grandfather Dream	37
Pussyboom, i.	37
Wasabi Summer	38
Curry Love Dance (Baby, Baby, Baby)	40
On Missing: Part ii.	41
Peninsula Park Rose Garden, Aug., 2014	42
A Hometown	42
6-Word Stories (iii.)	42
Tequila Bones	43
I Hope You, Hope You, Hope	46
Probably Foolish (& More Than a Little Vain)	47
On Missing Part iii.	47
The Storm	48
Breakdown Narratives	50

If I Were a Honeybee ... 53
Fucked Up & Majestic ... 54
6-Word Stories (iv.) ... 54
Wish You Were Here ... 55
Let It Sink ... 56
The Way Martyrs Say Prayers ... 57
My Father is Appalachia Noun ... 58
To My Sister on Her 30th. Birthday ... 59
Old Yeller ... 62
Pussyboom, ii. ... 63
For Ashley, Who I Have Loved ... 64
To Call You Persephone ... 67
The Year I Graduated High School ... 68
When the Monster Takes Your Knees ... 68
Natural Disaster ... 69
Isn't Technically A Kiss ... 70
Last Person to See ... 71
Raindrops & The Sound of Ghosts ... 73
When The Doctor Asks ... 74
Speaks Beaten Dog Fluently ... 74
Oh, To Be a Young Johnny Depp ... 75
Remember Four Yrs. Old, Arizona Sunlight ... 76
A Girl I've Learned To Kiss ... 77
Because Your Body Was a Roadside Fruitstand ... 78
Pussyboom, iii. ... 80
I Asked the Spine of a Book ... 81
The History of Tonight ... 81
A Charm, A Troubling ... 81

Five from 2016–2018:

When I Asked You to ... 86
How to Choose the Perfect Avocado ... 87
On that Couch in the Yard, At the Edge of Adulthood ... 88
You Cast Yourself into the Desert, Where There is No Air ... 89
Geode Heart/Break ... 90

Index of first lines ... 92
About the author ... 95

ROCK

PAPER

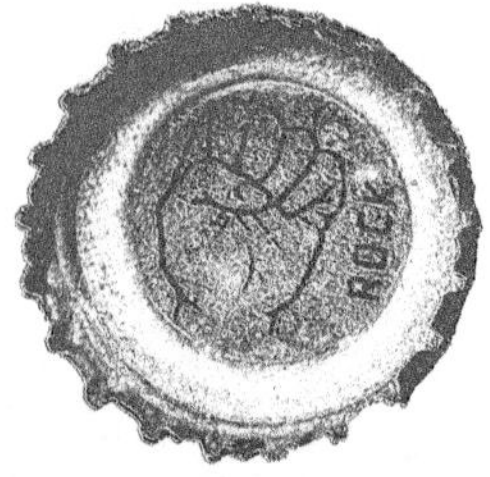

ROCK

POVERTY

The first time I realize we are poor
my mother stands in the kitchen
    mixing water with magic; making
cake for dinner because
    there is no food. There
in the kitchen where
    we put dawn in
the dishwasher. My mother:
    a child with children. we
waded through bubbles
    for a day. Everything soft,
everything floating. Laughter.
            There

was laughter in that kitchen,
    but no food. My mother
stoop-shouldered with a wooden spoon
    mixing pre-packaged alchemy
into something for our bellies.
    German chocolate cloyingly
sweet, sticking to the ribs

    where the laughter lived.
The ache like hunger. The
    ache like something too-
sweet kicking in your teeth.
    We frost it with our bare hands,
the cake we'll make last
    until the next government
subsidy. The first time
    I realize

we are rich, we are rich
    like chocolate cake for dinner.
Barefoot with my mother
    in that kitchen, soft and floating,
full of laughter.

BECAUSE MY FATHER WAS A MOUNTAIN MY MOTHER COULDN'T MOVE

Because my father was a mountain my mother couldn't
                                        move,
        she hollowed her tunnel veins for
our swollen hearts to pass through. Stretched her bones like
        telephone wire
        so we could speak around his silence.

                She hollowed her tunnel veins,
        but our swollen hearts never learned the language of
        compression.
So. We could speak around his silence
        or bind our tongues in Appalachian snow, winnowing

our swollen hearts. Learn the language of compression:
        tin cans strung between bedroom windows.
Bind our tongues in Appalachian snow? Winnow
        thin strands of history. From the

    tin cans strung between bedroom windows
our swollen hearts might pass through. Stretched: her bones
like telephone wire
        (thin strand of history. Of heritage.).
Because my father was a mountain, my mother couldn't
                                        move.

AFTER
EACH WAR

After each war:

I counted my teeth
        as coup to prove
I existed

        as more than the rattle
                in your hands
        after one-too-few
vodka tonics

INCHWORM LULLABY

When I was young
            my mother measured
the length of these limbs
            in lullabies,
fingers gliding over dimpled
                        baby skin, singing
      inchworm/inchworm,
                  measuring the marigolds.

   My mother was 21
                  the year chemicals birthed rapture
      the year her friend
                  birthed a corpse. The year
my mother gave birth
                  to her own Dead End
she called me 'daughter'.

            When I was young
                  my mother traced roadmaps
      into the canvas of my skin,
                        labeled each landmark –
Declared my fists two sovereign nations.
      Named my kneecaps redemption.
                  She called my spine Pangæa,
prayed I'd always feel whole.

My mother
      was postcards at summer camp
and unwrapped birthday presents
                  because she didn't
trust herself with scissors.
            My mother was 21 years old
                  the year crystal bloomed

behind the spackled rind
                        of her iris One Last Time;
the year we cried
                for six months because
our bellies were full with
                        sharp edges.

        When I was young
                        my mother had artist hands
    and on the days they rattled
                                like a dying breath
        I brought her my baby teeth
                                like peace offerings
            so she'd have something
    to cling to.

            My mother
                    was 26 years old when
she broke down: 100 lbs
                        in a hospital gown, her ribs
like the riveted doors of an
                    empty cupboard. My mother
                                was a ghost town
                or Christmas at the halfway house.
    She asked me to be origami,
                    folded me precisely into a
                            blue heron dream.
                Now she's the string I tie
                                to my finger
                so I never forget that
        "I love you" means stay
    a little longer.

            Means don't leave me.
                        I am not just the ghost

17

of her dream, I am a house
                    of new memories
              saying: stay.
     Stay with me.

WHETHER
YOU REMOVE A
BANDAID

      here is what i know:

               whether you remove
       a bandaid slowly or
               quickly, you are going
to lose skin. so come

     on, baby. dance with me
               once more and again
          before we remove
               'we' from our vocabularies.

THE
ART OF WAKING
UP

Every year with the predictability
   of seasons, my brother grows me a new
          crop of sleepless nights. His
body becomes grape vine: heavy
with cellular accumulation.

He incubates hard marbles of tissue
in the hollow of his throat (where
I keep my poems and memories).

       Imagine: surgeon's fingers delicately

    plucking

the ripe and rounded sickness from
   the tiny sleeping form. He handles the
tumors delicately, easily bruised fruit.
    He asks us if we'd like to see them, but
we don't. It's easier to imagine the
body as trellis, entangling green.

       My brother

was eleven and a half pounds at birth,
   his body graceless from the moment it
twisted fractured into this world.
      His bones learned the lesson
of contortion, cracking beneath
   the dual clench of pelvis
and gravity. He knew pain
   before he knew to breathe.

After each operation
   he teaches me the language
of blind faith, the art of waking up.
    His sleeping body
curls into itself like
   a question mark. I am
still looking for
    the answers.

I AM A KNOWN BREAKER OF BROKEN THINGS

I am a known breaker of broken things.
I can guarantee the permanent dismantling
       of anything even moderately salvageable.
While gluing the handle back on your
                              favorite mug?
I will undoubtedly manage to chip the rim.
      Patching your jeans I'll blow a seam
rendering them unwearable.
                         Listen.

Next time you're on your hands and knees
       digging through dust bunnies for those lost batteries.
You. Will. Regret. The day
      I offered to fix the remote control
because I inevitably manage to crack
            the plastic snap off the back,
                              that delicate tab meant to
            hold everything together.
I'm not the best at keeping it together.

      See, my dad was the guy who'd give you
a reason to cry if you couldn't supply
      a full alibi for every. Single. Tear.
Complaining about scraped knees or bee
      stings earned a two-fold return in the currency
of pain, teaching a younger me
                  the most efficient means
to overcome one agony
                  is replacing it with another.

I don't mean to be blunt
      but the force of trauma was the only lesson
I ever learned from love.
                    I will be a kick in the ribs
when what you needed was someone
                          to kiss it better.

Darling, I can see the seams
      where your delicate dreams are knitting
themselves
      back together.

                          So please.

Don't offer me those parallel lines,
      scar tissue rungs strung
                    across your upper thighs,
      the ladder you climb to escape
each personal hell.

Don't tell me the history of your body.
      Describe the trajectory and delicacy
of stick-thin child limbs,
                    plaster walls elastically
absorbing the full weight of you
      after mom had one-too-many
gin nightmares.

You are porcelain
      and these hands were tempered in concrete.
Your wings might be a bit bent (testament
      to the turbulence they underwent) but
                          they are healing.
Don't tempt me to fix you.
      I am a known breaker of broken things.

SIX-
WORD STORIES
(i)

I'm through writing letters to ghosts.

THE NIGHT
OUR FRIENDSHIP FELL DOWN
THE STAIRS

The night our friendship fell down the stairs
and died from internal complications:

Upon its final heartbeat I discretely wrapped
my clean white sheets around
          our shared past, neatly tucked it away
to complete the funeral rites
          in my kitchen (replete with euphemisms
and jello salad).

You ask why the good die young and
    I hold my tongue because it's
the right thing to do.
    Tater tot hot dish seals my mouth
like glue and I remember you
    once told me you
can't eat anything in casserole form
                              because the taste reminds you
of Death.

    Still I watched you drink yourself
to the brink every night
    and never think twice about
the taste of
    Dying.

Did it feel like flying? Your body
    complying to the gravity of reality,
my stairwell wreaking hell on your
    bruisable peach shell.

You said the pain
        reminded you of childhood.
Like that was a good thing.

This winter
    your features pulled tight against
their frame, roadmap veins painting
    the way to all your nameless insecurities.
Huddled in my living room

                        I hide behind dark lenses.
I tell you everyone has Daddy Issues.

You tell me to Fuck Off,
            slurred words hurled like
sticks and stones not to
            break my bones but to
    open my eyes.

    I reply with that threadbare lie:
It'll All Be Fine.

            What I mean is I Can't Fix This,
    so I mix us another drink
                and we sink back into that slow
blinking state of sleeping wakefulness.

            We wear dark glasses.
                Ignore the internal bleeding.
                Never eat casserole.

DOWN
BY THE BAY WHERE
LIGHTHOUSES

down by the bay
            where lighthouses i have
    never known rust
            in the chill quench of storms,
and our tin can hearts rattle
            cresting the final ascent,

    i sketch love into
            the low tide, while your
    blue coat skips stones
            into nimble islands. here
clear bottles hold saltwater
            like a message meant
    for drowning lips

 and unbroken birds hover
            like fevered dreams. take
    my hand in the sun
            and the rain and the fields
    of golden dune grass.

        don't let go.

MEET ME, LET ME

Meet me at
the unraveling–
your knees like
twin mountains
freckled with the
force of falling.

Let me whisper
canyon songs that
echo through the wild
of your tremble.

Let me raise
your sea level
until the city
pants, hot and alive
with the flood
of your unhinging.

TODAY AT THE BUS STOP

Today at the bus stop a
girl shared her umbrella with me.
I don't know
what poetry is
but it sounds
a lot like rain
against taut fabric.

SIX-
WORD STORIES
(ii.)

Be anything except indifferent towards me.

YEAR
OF THE
BEAR

i.

My body is an empty den.
  I have been somebody's
home, this marrow painstakingly
                carved to the contour
of her name.

ii.

The summer my tongue
    discovered the backside of your teeth
we dragged my mattress onto the floor
    to muffle the sound of our fucking.
                We wouldn't learn to make love
for three more months.

iii.

Your belly
    was a full bowl of milk
and I was lactose intolerant.

iv.

The last time
  I drank a Big Gulp soda:

driving 582 miles
south and west in my silly clown car.
The cup was too big for the holders,
I clutched it at least an hour.
When I pried my fingers off
the sweating plastic
they ached because
because, because,
they were still alive.
You are like that cup.

v.

I gathered my bones
like an offering and poured them
into the hollow collection plate
of your ribcage. You
taught me the word
"religion".

vi.

The first time
I thought I could save myself
I did it for you.
I imagine that's the closest
translation for "love".

vii.

When you called me on Christmas morning
I was hungover in an IHOP
avoiding eye contact
with the stranger I'd fucked
the night before.

            Back then she was friction
   but now she has a face
            I hold in both hands.
I say her name like a prayer

viii.

   You made my mouth
feel like an oyster.
            Like I was growing so many pearls
   I forgot this was
supposed to hurt.

ix.

I have been empty for so long now –
   knotted scar tissue hole collecting
debris and memories, longing for
      something to inhabit these cold walls.
Make yourself at home.

x.

we were bears:
   slick-bellied and hungry.
Lean in the way of things
   familiar with starving.

RAZOR
BLADES AND INDIA
INK

Razor blades and india ink
  on the bedside table, or her
sheets roughing up
            my scraped knees
when I wake up alone. I
  am lonely in a way
you would understand

if you were here.

She tells me the birds
  are only singing because it's spring.
They don't trouble themselves
            with weather the way I do.
They live the way I love,
  in seasons. It has been february
for years.

FUTSAL * IS NOT
RUGBY!

'futsal
    is not rugby'
the third foul
            indignantly intones
from the sideline

            while the last
ten minutes
            sneak off the
clock. they have
            places to be,

            after all.

*) *Futsal is an indoor 5v5 soccer played on a
smaller court w/ a smaller, weighted ball, &
apparently big in Brazil & Portland OR*

ALL YOUR
FACES LOOK THE
SAME

You tried to tell me purple was for hope –
    so I climbed inside and strip-mined
this life for every shard
        I had left to compress
            into this geode heart.

            These days all I do is bleed quartz,
        pressing slivers to my lovers' lips.
You told me miracles unfold in the hazy glow of
        Sunday mornings, in the gaudy stone
of dime store rings,
        or the round river rocks
                    that lined our pockets.
They never learned to skip
                    across moving water.

You were like moving water
        trapping years beneath your ribs –
low-slung hungry nights
        slumped heavy in your arms, heady
with the somehow chemical smell
            of undeveloped dreams.
You were always searching
        for a way to save each
hazy second lost to golden
            smog of minutes. Eternity unfurled
between each tock and tick
        of your pendulum heart.

                You broke your future and named it purple.

You told me wolfsong
                    was the voice of god. So I filled
my mouth with that hollow empty

sound, the sound of lonely
    sounds like purple.

On moondrunk nights our voices danced
    five steps to the left of so-clumsy feet.
When I wander these streets
        I fill my empty pockets with
reasons not to call you. They rattle
    through my fingers like baby teeth
or loose change.

    You tried to tell me purple was for hope –
the taste of morning's stumblestagger yawn,
    (like breath you held waiting for the sun)
face upturned. Arms outstretched.

    Praying, please, for purple.

ON
MISSING: PART
ONE

This morning
(I was buying an avocado
        in a store where
your cells have
        never been with the too
bright lights and the
        stale music and your
remembered laughter swarming
        an ambush, and
have you noticed how ripe
        the fruit has
been this winter? I
        am amazed I can
eat avocado without
        aching for your
summer-flecked shoulders,
        but I can. I do.)
I am overwhelmed
        with missing you.

LET'S SET OUT BEFORE THE SUN COMES UP, LET'S DRIVE THIS TRAIN WRECK IN-TO THE OCEAN

Let's set out before the
        sun comes up
travel east or west until
        we run out of east
or west.

Let's drive this train wreck
        into the ocean, hop
a barge that will take
        us to a new state of being.

Let's wash our sooty
        hands and faces, avoid
the burnt out places
        and be grateful —
we made it out alive.

        I never meant to play the arson.

Darlin' I was thirsty
        for death and you
were the nearest
        bottle of gasoline,
twist off the top
        and slop you down
my open throat.
        Wait for the spinning
to stop. A child

with a box of matches
I turned my insides to ashes
   and fancied myself
a phoenix.
   Now I'm learning we
               can't always
         rise again.

On the subject of friendly fire:
   I never meant to shoot you down.

WHEN
YOU MAKE
LEMONADE

In last night's shot glass
   mix equal parts regret and
don't-give-a-fuck.
   Pluck the fruit that looks most
            like the sun,

                    pretend the universe
could unbecome in your hands.

Carefully remove every seed.
   There's no need to grow
         any more bitter. Frost your tongue
                    with sugar, chew a hole
            through the rind like every
safety net you've designed
                your escape from.

   Squeeze. Repeat.

582
MILES

I wrote a poem and called it
     The Color of Your Eyes,
or maybe it was *Thunderstorms in August.*
          No. It was *Cornfield at Dusk.*
It was *Empty Highway in a Hailstorm*
               (and No End in Sight).
These are the phases of my mind:
     your dirty t-shirt crumpled in the corner
where bed meets wall,
          a ball of cotton and stale sweat.
If I held it to my face I could
               almost smell your laughter –
dizzy and a little drunk.
          Cheap beer and your
favorite perfume.

These words are dangerous, double agents
     smudged onto pages. I'm
documenting phases of this love
     like tides or moons:
an almanac of the past.
     Because we were never the
best predictors of weather.
          Short sleeves in a hailstorm,
welts worn like purple badges
               of honor or maybe stupidity.

Do you remember that morning:
               pineapple jam and
burnt toast? Ice like shattered glass
     littering the coast.

There's a fist in my chest
    clenched tight around that memory.
Your hands still grounding me,
            hurtling
    through space to that place
our futures diverged, the urge to reverse
        our trajectory. Shatter reality like
            ice on the shore, like hailstones
against concrete.
                Just keep driving.

I want to press my mouth to
    the center of your third eye,
want to memorize the taste
    of your ten fingertips pressed to my lips
so when my sanity slips,
    skips town and drifts 582 miles
West of Forever at least I'll remember
    the ways we used to fit together.

Instead I fill my mouth with your absence,
    mumble about hail and
cornfields and highways full
    of blue heron dreams. I crumple
myself in the corner like your
    dirty t-shirt, hoping to still fit
when we find our way home.

GRANDFATHER
DREAM

last night i dreamed
my grandfather's bare chest
his naked breasts heavy
with too many years.
the moon
surges tidal waves into
my waterlogged body,
beaches shipwrecks
in my throat, dislodging
artifacts i thought i'd lost
forever.
here, five mood rings
glowering purple.
a blue heron wing
and the scarlet cleft
of a fish's slit throat.
the moon
asks me to be full with her.
i swallow sea water

PUSSYBOOM,
1

leave your skin
on the bedroom floor.

ask the moon
how she lost her fullness –
in a flurry of hips
and hands. she
doesn't miss your mouth
like a window. she
never asked you
to open.

WASABI
SUMMER

The summer we were fucked up kids
    I replaced my fingerprints
with question marks and seared
    inquisitions into my lover's thighs.
I planted prayers behind my eyes
    like grains of sand, hoping to grow pearls
but all I ever yielded was a
    tendency to be rigid. Back

then there were days you became desert
    and I forgot to wear shoes.
I grew new calluses to traverse you.
    Now I am unraveling thick skeins
of scar tissue, because these nerve endings
                were forged iron by infernos.

I never realized
    I'd be running on dead feet,
pounding the beat of a quick retreat
    until you weren't there to
slow my frenzy, saying

        Baby.
Wait. You're missing it.
    The sun's right over there
dancing just for you.

And you were dancing just for me
    that winter in your bedroom,
Eagles blooming through the speakers
    and you: lip-synching with every
muscle in your body.

There's gonna be heartache tonight.

I know.

Because
sometimes pain is the only symptom
    of being alive. Sometimes our minds
become minefields while metal detector
hearts hang heavy in our chests
    Unwound clocks, gathering dusk.

I still remember my friend's face
    the day she lobbed a wad of wasabi
into her open mouth; swallowed it whole
    like a grenade, prayed it would singe
everything on the way down.

Across town
    there is a girl I am learning to kiss.
On nights like this I want to
    swallow her whole, unhinge my jaw
and feel her slide down my throat —
    an emotional bulimic I'll binge
on her secrets until I make myself sick.

Twenty years or days or minutes later
    I'll lose her in a spasm of regret
before I've had time to digest
    what it means to say, "I'll miss you".

You

    were the instant before I bit off
more than I could swallow.

Now I'm choking on the hollow
carcass of our history, fractured
        poems like chicken bones caught
in the folds of my throat.

    Imagine this body:
breaking at the seams,
        straining to contain all of this
perfect nothing.
    My stomach clenches tightest

                        around absence.

        I just want to feel full.

CURRY
LOVE DANCE (BABY, BABY,
BABY)

Press your cheek to my heart beating
        like a record on repeat:
                        baby baby, baby.

    Sink easily into this place with me.

Let's slow dance in the kitchen.
    These two left feet will do their best
to follow Sinatra's lead, a
        twirl and clumsy dip,
my lips stumbling over the lyrics.

Slip your fingers between mine.
    Press your kiss to my closed eyes
and breathe futures into laughing
        speculations on the implications
            of homemade curry, movies on the couch

and my mouth's inability to resist
                    your skin.

Come in, lover. This space
    between my chin and breasts was made for
your head to rest, let your breath
            paint shivers across my skin.
I feel your heart
            knocking across the doorway of my ribs.
    Come in.

ON
MISSING: PART
TWO

I'm sorry.
    I killed the african violet
                    you gave me that summer
    you almost believed in love

again.

                    (You
    wanted to give me something
                    purple, but hope was hard
        to come by that
                    year.)

    Nurturing is not my forté.

                    There is too much gray here
    for green and growing things.

**PENINSULA
PARK ROSE GARDENS,
AUG., 2014**

"hot wonder,
funny face. my
hero. sunrise/
sunset.

little mischief.
daydream."

**A
HOMETOWN**

you were a hometown:

something you either
grow into or
out of.

**SIX-
WORD STORIES
(iii.)**
Kiss me like keys kiss locks.

TEQUILA
BONES

I told you I loved you
         before I knew it was true.
             That summer smelled
     like cigarettes and cheap beer,
    like sweat and fear and lonely.
I had been drunk
      every day for six months
           the night we strapped
     your mattress to a jeep.
That night you asked to sleep
      in my bed, standing in my doorway.
    You were sad and lovely
      in a way that made me
   want to invent new words.

Last winter
  through a kitchen window
that would never be ours
  you showed me the place
you used to smoked cigarettes
      in your underwear.
Sometimes
  late at night I smoke cigarettes on my roof
feeling lonely for that girl I never knew.
  I want to tell her everything will be fine.
I want to believe everything will be fine.

  Two nights ago
the lights stretched below us,
    slow cars like sticky platelets

gliding through the city's veins.
                    We seared solar flares into our lungs
let smoke stun the swarm of truths
            trapped beneath our tongues.
        I didn't mean to laugh
                but we're constantly
    halfway between
            tragedy and comedy.

    Yesterday.
    You held me like a baby
while I wept, knees to chest,
            my face pressed
into the crease of your neck.
        You asked my why I'll always choose the rain
                    and I can't explain except
            I keep hoping it will help me
    appreciate the sun.

When I was young
    I slept with my feet uncovered
so I could run through my dreams.
    I'd cling to my bedpost so
I never lost my way back.
    Now I sleep
holding onto the pieces of myself
    I'm most afraid of losing,
dig fingertips into my own ribs
    as if I could knit myself back together.
You told me you'll always be there
            when I need to find my way back.
But you are not mine to look for anymore.

Tomorrow.
    I will leave this town.
And when the plane banks low
        over the snow covered peak
                        of Mount Hood
    I won't remember the way
your forehead tastes
        every time I'm kissing you goodbye.

    Imagine me somewhere.
Imagine me peaceful.
    Don't check in.
I don't want to disappoint you again.
    I might call you home
and you call me best friend
        but in the end they're just different words
                        for "never".

    Tomorrow.
                I'll go back to the places
        where gravity feels lightest.
                I'll remember how to sleep again,
        remember dreams without you in them.
                        I used to laugh
            when you talked about going back to Real Life
    like somehow we could slip
                in and out of reality
the way you put on a winter jacket
                to survive the worst of the cold.
    I'm not laughing anymore.

                Last year
                    in the winter tomb of your bedroom

you asked what I want to be
                when I Grow Up, and I'm sorry I lied
when I laughed and said "Alive".
                See, I want to be a star.
        Or the idea of a star;
                something you can wish on.
        A spinning supernova
                that implodes far away
        and in its ultimate act
                of self-destruction
        finally attains beauty.

I HOPE
YOU, HOPE YOU,
HOPE

"i hope your skeletons
        found somewhere else
to rest their bones, i

        hope your closet holds
nothing but shoes
        and clothes. i hope you

have no use for
        nooses

because this world
        leaves you breathless
    with beauty."

PROBABLY
FOOLISH (AND MORE THAN
A LITTLE VAIN)

it is probably foolish
        (and more than a little vain)
to hold the contents of this body
                    in such high regard –
frothy gold spun industriously
        from the bluegreen seams
of my arm.

        but on the nights
i am heavy with dark
        i press my fingertips to each
throbbing artery and marvel
        at the sunshine coursing
through my being,

            holding everything together.

ON
MISSING: PART
THREE

You and I

        We never watched scary movies
                    produced later than the 80s.
        You had enough nightmares already,
and I only had these two arms.
        Terror has so many faces
but these days
        each one has your name.

These days I sleep
        wearing more purple
                than you could imagine
        so don't try.
    Don't try, ok?
    Don't try.

THE
STORM

The house hunkers low
    shutters latched, cupboards stacked
with cans, fresh water and
    an infinite supply of Tang, because
if we're going to be astronauts
        my god we're going to do it right!

        We consider ourselves stoic,
watch the storm grow,
    deepening into a sickly green
like a darkening bruise or how I
    imagine our hearts must look
after 8 months of abuse.

            When the tornado finally hits
    we're ready,

ready to be tugged from this
    gray Kansas love,
            and flung into
that Technicolor dream world –
    Someday

Raindrops like river rocks
    pelt the clapboard, shatter windows
like buckshot or cannon fire.

  We dig our stubborn fingers
      into the floorboards the way
                          that house clings
          to its rocky foundation,
      waiting.

I want to yell "It's not working!"
      But in the din my words begin
to sound like "Don't leave me!"

So we scramble madly,
            dismantling what we'd
built: memories thrown overboard,
    bailing out the husk of the house
like water from the bottom of a boat.
Not to keep us afloat but to
    make us light enough for flight.

I start with the Christmas mugs.
      The pictures in their mismatched frames.
Trinkets and love notes, the pocket
    full of mood rings

(still proclaiming "romantic"
      when all I ever felt was blue).

 We tear off the shutters,
                    pry up the floorboards,
heave the refrigerator into
    the eye of the storm and then

finally. It's just you and I
shaking in the wake of
our own destruction.

I know you said "I'm sorry"
as you wrenched open the door.
But I could have sworn
it sounded just like
"I love you."

BREAK-
DOWN NARRATIVES

Tuesday
The fault lines of your mother's breakdown begin to
echo through your hollow bones,
your blood aches heavy with heredity
and slivers of purple.
Your hands will tremble for a
hundred years or more.

Wednesday
When the infection begins to spread, don't panic.
Amputate and cauterize
before the gangrene enters the bloodstream.
Your heart will look
smaller than you expected,
laid out like a dead kitten
on the exam table.
Disregard the girl
lodged in the left ventricle.

Thursday
Time becomes mutable.
   You might be cork floating,
a pulpy clot in the
   cheap red liquid, you replace
your blood with gasoline
   and search for a match.
You drink your dinner
   and dream of feasts.

Friday
   Pack memories into heavy
bodybags. Carry them beneath your eyes.
         Remember laying your body
across the linoleum,
         how she chewed the brittle crust
from the salted rim of your hipbone,
   lapped tequila from the basin of your navel.
As the alcohol slid down your naked sides
         you thought about open heart surgery,
wondered about the cavity
   inside your chest.

Saturday
You want to ask the girl at the bar
   if she found the poems you tucked behind her teeth.
Her stranger's hands rattle over
   each knot of your spine,
you could be the ladder she climbs
   into ecstasy.
Your whiskeyheavy breaths
   are prayers of deliverance,

in the morning
	her naked back will be a foreign country
you explore with eyes/hands/mouth.

Sunday

	Trace origami lines into your
arms and thighs so you never again forget
		where to fold.
The moon surges tidal waves through your frame,
			lodges shipwrecks (heavy with artifacts)
in the cove of your throat. There:
	5 mood rings spitting purple,
a blue heron wing, the
		scarlet cleft of a fish's slit belly.
The moon asks you to be full with her.
		Swilling down seawater, you
	are left gasping.

Monday

You know the purple orange glow
	of the night sky is just city light
refracted off the low-slung clouds
	but that instant it could be god.
Your mouth aches for butterscotch
	but only tastes smoke and lighter fluid,
your lungs are low-slung clouds,
	heavy with god and apocalypse.

Tuesday

	Self-inflicted wound begins
		to peel and flake.
			Lodge the memory
	beneath your nail beds.

You are growing a new skin,
days woven into spiderweb scar tissue.
Under the shower head, your sorrow
leaves you cleansed.
Grind saltwater exfoliant into
both cheeks and hope
to wake fresh-faced in the morning.

Wednesday
Splay your puzzle piece body
across purple sheets and
dare a stranger to cobble you
into her bloodstream.
Press your tongue against her scars
and wonder what she burned for,
press your stories into her palms
like offerings. Like prayers.
You tell her you're a narcissist.
You tell her you've almost died twice.
You tell her, and tell her and tell and tell and...

IF I WERE
A HONEYBEE

if i were a honeybee
i'd be a sting, something
soon forgotten. but you

you are the death
of me.

FUCKED UP AND
MAJESTIC

i am a fucked up
              majestic little
universe. here
              the eternity of a
heartbeat. here
              a bounding pulse
against scarred
              fingertips. here a
galaxy of implosion
              unravelling into elastic
     supernovas.

              this clumsy
unravelling won't
              birth a demise. this
     brief eternity –

              held like breath
under glass ribs,
              makes the starscape
of my solar system hips
              pant electric.

SIX-
WORD STORIES
(iv.)

Even my silence knows your name.

WISH
YOU WERE
      HERE

The city
   is wearing
   your eye color again
                     inappropriate
like a christmas cardigan
                  in july. Stifling.

when the man on the corner
   asks for change
               I describe the
                     inside of your elbow –
crisscrossed highways
                  of anatomy, how you always
stretched the boundaries
                  of your skin.

I promise the sidewalk
                  to leave unlucky pennies
   where they lie if its cracks
                  will stop resembling
your hands. Life lines
                  like water spilling to the
                     edge of each palm.

   I don't know how to talk
                     about your kneecaps,
the gravity of your slapdash mouth.
                     your two eyes looking at her
   like water. My two eyes
                  looking at you the same;
   or your name
               under my tongue. The
                  biggest lie I ever told.

**LET
IT SINK**

When the miles
          get caught in your throat:
imagine your grandfather's
          hands before they shook
pouring coffee, or the slick
     oil sheen shimmying
  over your grandmother's
               skillet. How air becomes

  heavy, moves so slowly
          in the moments between
words. Like it could hold
          memory the way your
  house holds lilacs in
          the spring. Purple teeming
from the least likely
          places.

  Swallow your pulse
          like a vitamin, let it
  sink into your belly
          and still your hands,
shaking over coffee. Over
          cigarettes smuggled from
  a stranger's apartment.
               Over thin wrists and thickly
  lined palms. Breathe.

THE
WAY MARTYRS SAY
PRAYERS

i want you

to say my name
　　　the way martyrs say
prayers:
　　　　　　like i'd be something
　　　worth dying for.

that's fucked up.

57

MY
FATHER IS APPALACHIA
NOUN

My father is Appalachia *noun*
        see also: native to poverty
      see also: frostbitten boychild
    see also: winterrooted
red nose. The constant
dripdripdip
of cold staining

    his shirtsleeves.
    Drowning in the
    thickspit mucus of
          History Runs Thicker
          Than Family
  but not nearly as
    fast or far. My father,
an orphan twice over,
    bred a legacy of bastards
bearing his features
  and tendencies.

He called me from her
deathbed three months
  before she died saying
      Goinggoinggone. I only
saw him cry once:
      sitting at the kitchen table
I said Going.
    Going.
    Going.
And I went.

TO MY SISTER ON HER 30th. BIRTHDAY

This is not a story.
This is four days
    of snow like a stifled scream
that's left me reeling. Sick
    drone dull ache buzzing
with the colony collapsing; left
        grasping toward common
    history.

    This is the darkest dream.
I never meant to grieve
    in a divulging heave of tequila –
chocolate cake and migrations,

    This is the final migration
we made, too afraid
    of becoming our father
or our mother's daughters
        to stay in that place.

Growing up we were the kids
    with names for
crosses on roadsides.
    Bottles in the backseat
rattling like ghosts preparing
    to take the stage. Regretting
each sharp turn we'd make:
    eyes closed, bones light, tongues
heavy with another night of
        maybe tomorrow.

Sorrowful. Like two cars

        keeping lonely company
on winterslick roads, banking
        on our own tenacity
to guide us home.

    I'm sorry.

When I saw my exit
        I took it. Left you alone
to navigate by the kaleidoscope
        glow of broken promises.

Thank god you flared so bright
        the sun had to close his eyes
when you looked him in the face
        and prayed for blindness.
And you never reflected
        that darkness like some hapless moon.
You just kept moving forward,
        because what else is there?

This is not a story
        like the year I invented monsters
to keep you out of my room
        when we both knew our father
was the only ghost
        haunting the halls of our heredity.

We grew up on the wrong side
        of the track lines in our mother's arms.
Driving cars that started maybe
        every fifth time. Understanding the crime
of taking "too much" at supper time meant
        listening to the family's hunger
rattle the floorboards.
        There is nothing romantic
                about being poor.

And I'm sorry
              for all the days we spent hungry.
Black rabbits in the mesh cage
              of winter's frostbite belly.

I am so proud of you.

                    How you grew
into this beautiful human being
                    with two hands full of scars;
barbed wire bands on both arms
                    from when your body learned a
      lesson in falling.

                    Now I should be calling you
as the blinking clocks stretch into
                    too long night, but instead I write
      by winter's glow:

      "This is not a story."
for the boys like stray dogs
      with their split lip smiles, or the miles
between holidays, nostalgia sharpened
      by hangover maladies.
This is quite simply a way
      for me to say "stay with me."
I love you like
      balloons love the wrists
they are tethered to. Too much
                    atmosphere makes me blue anyways.
   Keep me grounded in these
      common roots.

            I love you.
   This is not a story.

OLD
YELLER

When I was a child there was
    a particular breed of movie scene,
something you'd see in Old Yeller
    or The Yearling. Gut-wrenching: equal
    parts horror and tragedy. Particularly, this:

a boy, shaking, cradling a gun
    preparing to kill someone he loved
in the name of growing up.

Forgive me this trigger-happy history
    but I was raised to believe
that love goes out with a bang.
    That's why I've put a bullet
in the brain of every relationship
        at the first sign of sickness, in
    the interest of self-preservation.

The problem is I have terrible aim.
    The problem is love takes so long to die.
The problem is that trigger sound still
    keeps me up at night. It sounds like
pouring that last drink; like my skin
    on a stranger's sheets. Or a silence
            stretching across the years
    still ringing.

Ringing.

    There is no such thing
as a mercy killing.

There are only boys with trembling hands
    learning that once love turns on you,
it doesn't matter what you've been through
    together. It will chew through your corn crib ribs
                        to ravage the beating heart within
    if you can't
fire

    first.

I'm sorry it's taken me so long to learn
    that love is not a rabid dog. Safety is
                        more than a thing to be turned off.
I'm still learning the difference between
    distemper and a bad day, so please be patient.
When I tell you I am afraid
    I mean I am unarmed.

I am bringing you my shaking hands
    and this beating heart. I am learning
        a language softer than gun, unloading
    this buckshot tongue, and praying
you don't tear me apart.

PUSSYBOOM,
2

            and
        in the morning
                the crows have turned
    to seagulls, sirens wailing
                the green sap from my bones.

FOR ASHLEY, WHO I HAVE LOVED

There is a girl back home
   who smells like powdered sugar.
Her lips are a berry patch
   in the middle of summer.
When she kissed me,
   it tasted like whiskey
and childhood. Her mouth
   like an open field of grain,
small straight teeth planted like
   mile-markers for my tongue
                    to follow.

   The first boy she ever loved
was her childhood friend
   and I never really knew him
but I like to pretend he was soft-spoken,
   with the tanned-hands of a
Montana farm boy,
             lean like a long drive
on back country roads.

   On the nights
I was a jukebox
   she knew all my saddest
songs. She always sang along with
   her eyes closed like she
could open them somewhere
                    far away.

Back then we were always afraid.
   Of becoming our fathers
or our mothers' daughters

or just more fodder for the
every day traipsing,
   clueless, into the future.

                    I have loved her.

   On the nights my thoughts stretch
thinner than the moonbeams
   we used to hold like prayers
I want to tell her:
   don't ever let them
get you down. You are
   more than the small town
parades and grass stains
   that you carry in your
                    veins.

You are not the
   plunder of the wars you
survived –
   you are the country
they were fought in, and even
      on the days you can't take
a breath that doesn't
         feel like lost ground
your hands are a roadmap.
            Your heart is a full tank of gas,
your smile is 500 miles
            of open road.

There is a boy out there
   who didn't show you
how to break, but how to
   shake the dust from
the rubble of each

mistake and shape
something beautiful from
          the clay you create.

I know
   you fancy yourself
a sand castle, but I've
   seen you stand solid
in the face of more
   waves than you
realize. Stay alive.
   Keep drinking in those
big blue skies like
      Lake Missoula wouldn't
satisfy your thirst.

   You are not the first
girl I have loved. I'm not
   the first kiss you whispered
across a fevered cheek
   like a promise. But I think
about you when the sun shines
                  just-so and I think you should know,
you are beautiful
   like red wine in a mason jar.
And on the nights I'm
   a jukebox
tossing love songs like rocks
   against the window
            of the moon

I still spill ablutions
   across the ground of every
new hometown, hoping you've
            found some semblance of peace.

TO
CALL YOU
PERSEPHONE

i want to call you persephone.
    i'm asking you to justify spring.
rewrite my history in the vast green
    expanse of you. please. become the
reason for this unfurling because
               god knows

there were enough nights i coaxed
    bloody beads like pomegranate seeds
from the seams of this body. i
    left them glistening on my lovers'
tongues like prison sentences.
    i wove my breath into their
tangles like promises. like shackles.

    darling, hades has been strumming
these heartstrings in the key of grief
    for too long. so i am rising from this
pit with hell on my heels,
    with the river styx dripping from
all ten fingertips to let you know:

    freedom
has been a myth for so long.

             but your hands look just like keys.

THE YEAR
I GRADUATED HIGH
SCHOOL

the year i graduated high school
i was raped

on four occasions
by 6 different bodies.

this life is full of sharp edges
and i will myself hard, will myself iron

but this flesh will always be clay
(warm. malleable.) under all the wrong hands.

WHEN
THE MONSTER TAKES
YOUR KNEES

when the monster
takes your knees
learn to pray on your back,
dig toes into thick slabs
of lovers' calves. Dig fingertips
into her wrist. Wrench your
pulse from between
her gasping thighs.

Take it back.

NATURAL DISASTER

How long does it take a letter
  to cover 176 miles
from you to me? 'Celebration'
  stamped across the front:
an explosive irony, bittersweet.
  like tongue in cheek. Like winks
are still kinda creepy, especially
            between friends. I tell you

  'a tornado will always
be a tornado' which means
  your smile is a natural
disaster I'm stockpiling
  supplies to survive. Or maybe
it doesn't mean that at all.
  You are beautiful and
dangerous.

What I'm trying to say is
  after my friend Sara's
grandfather died they
  found rolls of money tied with tight
twine knots in bags of dried
  beans. crammed between
the floorboards that creaked beneath
     three generations of sun hardened
men. Hidden in the ceramic hen he

gave her grandmother on their
twenty-seventh wedding anniversary.
   This is how you survive
the greatest depressions:
   sucking thick yellow marrow
from cracked bones because
   you don't know when your
next meal will come. So
   forgive me for clinging
to your words like offerings; for
            weaving your freckled lips
into the fiber of my dreams.

   I can see the storm coming
like a letter crossing state lines.
                  I am just trying to survive.

ISN'T TECHNICALLY A KISS

   a hickey
         isn't technically a kiss
but i leave them
         on your skin to feel
               some sense of permanence.
         they'll fade

   after a handful of days
               but I hope to remain
         there:

                    nestled just under
          your collarbone
               when you are
                         far away.

**LAST
PERSON TO
      SEE**

               I was the last person to see you alive:
     bloodied nose in a dive bar bathroom stall
                         hands like chaliced claws
     cupped to accept your body's offering.

               Back then
          we measured booze
                    in fists instead of fingers,
          swinging cheap shots
                    at anyone who dared to love us.
     I guess not much has changed.

               The first time
          I almost lost my front tooth
                    I thought I was superman after
     downing a can of 4 Loko in
                    your jeep's back hatch. You tried
          to catch me on the way down
                    but I was so sure I could fly:
     arms at my sides, chin stretched
                    skyward. You carried me inside
     after I knocked myself unconscious.

          The first time I almost broke my back
I mixed a rack of PBR with
                    a friend's trampoline straining
   to be airborne. I didn't see
                    the ground coming until it was knocking
the breath out of me. World spinning
                    at speeds my creaky knees
         could never hope to achieve.

These bones
         have always ached to be hollow.
                    So I swallow cheap liquor. It
   makes my tongue thicker but my head
                    feels light like the balloons
we'd cling to at childhood birthday parties.

         Remember when we tied strings to our wrists,
wistfully longing to overcome gravity?
                    Never realizing we were merely
         tethering otherwise free things.

   I was the last person to see you alive,
                    nose bleeding apologies the way
   my apologies bled ignorance. And in that
                    instant I swear I loved you

      the way homeless men
                 love park benches.
   The way injuries love crutches.
                 The way our lungs love their next breath.
Which is to say "incidentally".
                 Out of necessity.

You were the next breath
I couldn't accept gracefully,
            and after you leave I won't
remember the exact press
            of my hand against your cheek
but I imagine it's the way
            gravity cradles airplanes –
going against my nature
            to keep you aloft.

RAINDROPS AND THE SOUND OF GHOSTS

raindrops and the sound of ghosts
    have followed me around this city
all fucking day. they pant and shrug
around my ankles like tired children
    who have long since forgotten
what they were begging for.

WHEN
THE DOCTOR
ASKS

When the doctor asks
    if I have allergies
I laugh and say
    'everything' because its safer
than missing something.

this world
    has been slowly
killing me since my body
    first recognized oxygen
as just another airborne
        pollutant.

SPEAKS
BEATEN DOG
FLUENTLY

    my co-worker
speaks
    beaten dog
fluently (the
    downcast
eyes, the grovelling
    lilt, statements
        up-spoken while
volume drops
    lowlowlow),
and somehow
    i find
myself

wanting to
    kick her
too.

OH,
TO BE A YOUNG JOHNNY
DEPP

today

   i want to be
      a young johnny depp
         smoking a cigarette
       cross-legged on the
train tracks, sweat and
       sun plastered to my
  forehead. i want

   to glare, shoulders
        hunched against the
    junction
  of here and
   nowhere (
      let the scissored hands of time shear this life
              like fine angora

    past and
   future
). Before
     the fear *&* loathing,
  before the loss of
every self-

  ish-

ness. evaporating like
    tracks on a horizon,
         (imagine smoke) cocks
    one finger. beckons
  you closer.

REMEMBER FOUR YEARS OLD, ARIZONA SUNLIGHT

                remember
four years old, arizona
        sunlight baking the smooth
desert of pale baby flesh. you
        are learning to be hardened clay.
you are standing in your backyard.

                remember
damp clutch of soiled cotton
        panties wadded in small fists,
familiar cartoon faces stained
        and heavy with panic.

                remember
the dark-haired girl
                with mop top curls.
                        how she always

        ended up on the wrong side
of his fine line?

                        you can't remember
        her name, but you remember
                        the precise weight of her urine
balled in the palm of your hand.

                        you can't remember
                                anything but the heavy
                press of his punishment,
the crime of biology against
                        your body.

don't try to remember.
    the dark-haired girl –
        afterwards
        she cried for you.

you can't remember
        his face. but the year
he gets out of prison his family
        invites you to join them in celebration.

your mother weeps on the kitchen floor.
        your memory is flooded with ammonia.
            your hands are suddenly damp.

A GIRL
I'VE LEARNED TO
KISS

there is a girl i've learned to kiss,
    trapping her tongue between my teeth
        like fresh fruit, or not like that at all.
            her hand feels confused in mine
    like it doesn't know how it
        came to be there.
she throws her head back
    when she laughs.
i let the sound
    rattle through me.
in the morning
    her naked back will be a foreign country
i explore with eyes/hands/mouth.
            i taste her scars
      and wonder when they
        finally stopped hurting.

BECAUSE YOUR BODY WAS A ROADSIDE FRUIT STAND

Today
I ate my first peach
    since you died.

The flesh
    was bitter and unyielding
like my memories of you,
    like before your body
was overripe fruit. Before
    you grew a hard pit of cancer
where you used to house
                    a lung.

    The last time I saw you
in a memory of a dream: three
    nights ago blowing bloody
bubbles in shallow water.
    Now every cigarette
is heavy with a breath
    you never got to take.
The last time I saw you

    alive

I was graduating college.
    Your mouth was a horizon
or a knife blade. Something
    equal parts sharp and indistinct,
like when you said you were proud
    but what would I do with my degree?

I didn't have an answer then.

I don't have an answer now,
that's why I write around you
like a game of musical chairs.
When the music stopped, one
of us had to sit down.

The last time we spoke
I was leaving home on
ice-slick country roads,
Christmas morning. I said I
had to go, but I'd talk to you soon.

The last thing I asked for
was your address, your last request
was more time, now I'm trying
to decompress the pressure
of so many words left unsaid.
So many hurts left unmended.

You are dead.

And while I thread my car
through rush hour traffic,
gouge my teeth through pulp
and rind the weight of memory
give beneath my incisors.

I'm sorry I kept you waiting.
I swear I meant to write.

PUSSYBOOM,
3

                    i don't know
            the circumference
                        of the earth

or the exact number of
                    people housed in the
expansive girth of her ribs,

                        we colorful cultures flaunting
            our tongues toward
                        the atmosphere.

                    but i know
            i love you from
                        the constellation of your
            earlobes to the toes
                        of the soft-soled feet
you twine around mine
                        in sleep. and if prayer

        were a language i'd
                    be fluent in the way you sigh
when our dreams collide.

I ASKED THE SPINE OF A BOOK

i asked the spine of a book
'teach me a lesson?'
and heard 'opening
is not the worst way to crack'

THE HISTORY OF TONIGHT

with the history of tonight
splashed purple (like the voice of god)
across the canvas of her torso–
she could be a murderer
or a homicide victim. nobody's
quite sure yet.

A CHARM, A TROUBLING

A group of hummingbirds is called a charm
or a troubling. In the dingy glow
of Thursday night the girls
resemble jeweled birds.
They hover endlessly–
darting from lap to lap. From
booth to rack to bar to booth.

81

Perched at the end of the bar,
    Rosie bats heavy lashes
while I slapdash vignette flashes
        of her charming companions:

Taylor flings her body with alarming trajectory,
            trusts solely the reliability of gravity.
She slams her hips into the rack,
            knows bruises won't erase the past.
But they justify the way she aches.

  Vegas drapes
        a heavy bandolier across
her childish hips.
                She fancies herself warrior
        but when she spreads
        her matchstick slender thighs
all the men see is combustion.

Ana didn't like the stars
            she was born under
        so she created new constellations:
blue ink tracings wound around her body
    the way she twines, serpentine,
                around the pole.

Suddenly, leering too close, a bearded face
    floats above a white-collared shirt
and (attempting to flirt) asks
        when my audition is. His
grin feels more entitled to my body
            than I have ever been.

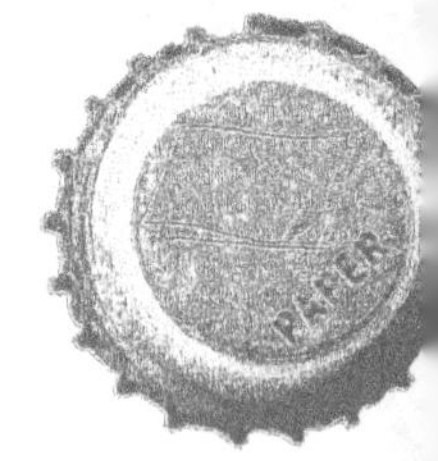

Rosie takes the stage. A
                    practiced actress, mask in place,
     face carefully arranged
                    into perfect impassivity.
                              Her naked breasts are a
                    gift
               my eyes have not yet
                         learned to accept,
          so I memorize her faces.
     When she bites her lip
               I taste blood.

     She once told me time is a myth
     that ceased to exist in a room
with no clocks and only mirrors
          where windows once thought they belonged.
Through the red room she flutters and twirls,
     black fabric swirls framing her thighs.
               She says the frills make men cry "Princess".

She confesses her desire to kick up sunbeams
     instead of puppeteering heartbeats.

                    Outside

          she says a pretty girl never lights
her own cigarette.
          So I ignite the flimsy tip,
     filter dangled between candied lips.
Smoke drips from the downturned
               corners of her kiss.
I want to collect it like water in my cupped hands,
     take it into my own mouth

to feel cleansed.
Or whole.
Or closer to home.

At sunrise she will shed her altered ego:
trades heels for ballet shoes,
thread her fingers through my belt loop.
We'll weave dizzily into
dawn;
my shoulders will grow new freckles
in the sun while she spins haphazardly
through the trees, the
bruises on her thighs fading
like last night never existed.
Like tonight will never come too soon
the way it always comes too soon.

The Hummingbird exhales the red room,
fills her tiny ribcage with spring,
and dances our hearts less heavy.

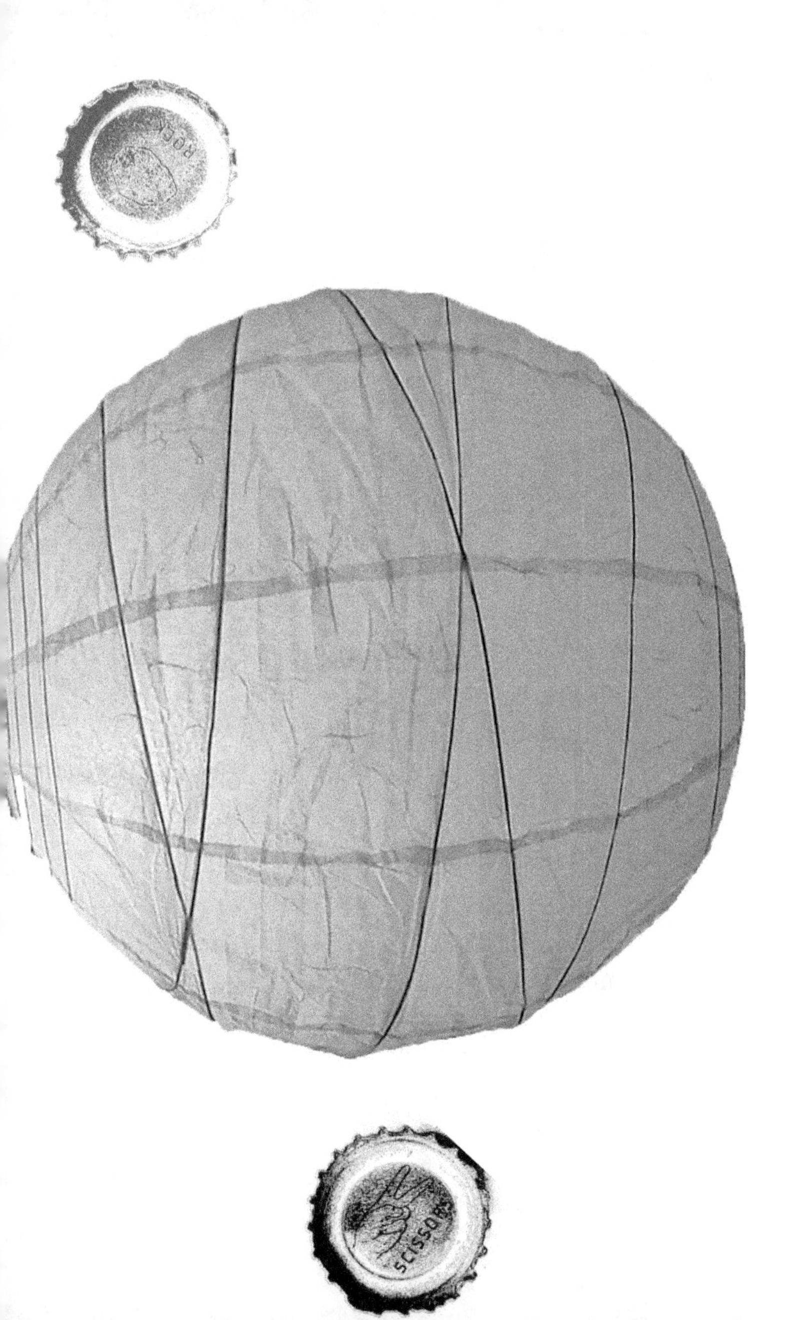

FIVE FROM

**WHEN
I ASKED YOU
TO**

when i asked you
        to fuck me
               i meant to say
    there is shrapnel
       in my lungs from
            every time I swallowed
                  her name like a
hand grenade.

           she told me the hardest part
about loving a bomb
    is nobody has any
           sympathy for your injuries.

       she told me 'the
hardest part about loving you
           is loving you'.

    when i asked you
to fuck me
      i meant treat my heart
like a snake bite. split
         open my chest, use
           your deft tongue and lips
              to siphon toxins
from my bloodstream

                              but please. don't
                              swallow.
                I can't be responsible for
another casualty.

HOW
TO CHOOSE THE PERFECT
AVOCADO

Last year you tried to teach me
how to choose the perfect avocado.

"See?" you said, twisting off the hardened
knot of stem to check the fruit for readiness.

I still scour the produce department for evidence
you may have left. I want to tell you some habits

don't come easy.

I want to tell you I am still wrong more
often than I am right and I still

fill my mouth with the brown and rot of this.
There are some lessons you can't learn or teach.

When the fruit is ripe, I eat.

ON THAT COUCH IN THE YARD, AT THE EDGE OF ADULTHOOD

On that couch in the yard, at the edge of adulthood,
    you told me that falling is the laziest way to gain
        admiration.

    Still we tried to catch stars with our outstretched hands,
children making grown up plans and

I swear I am trying to be brave but it's February, and the
                city is
    shaking off snow like the sweat from a wet dream, sap
        crackling

    like clotted honey in the trees' yawning veins, so I take
        two shots
of whiskey at the corner dive bar. The scars, like stars, fade

in early dusk. Bring me your back bent double with lonely.
    I'll show you my tongue full of knots. I am tired of
                                    being

    a mirror when you are looking for a window.
Please, won't you teach me how to open?

YOU CAST
YOURSELF INTO THE DESERT WHERE THERE
IS NO AIR

You cast yourself into the desert
        where there is no air. There you
                wander sixty days and nights.
        The sun blisters your feet into callous.
The heat frosts your lips with chap.

                Your forsaken promised land,
        I sorrow myself fifteen pounds more
as if to fill the space you left.
I break bread with the demons
        but remain unfed. I fatten the calves
                for an empty feast and dream
                        of your gnashing sleep-toothed grin.

I've heard when you lose a lung
        The other lobe grows like
                a grotesque carnival goldfish
                        to fill the cavity. Are you breathing
                just for one like me?
        Does the loss leave you gasping?

                I grow full with the moon and the missing.
        When you come home I will have no need
of pilgrims nor supplicants.

GEODE
HEART/BREAK

Some days
I am afraid of the way
my skin begs for her affection,
her fingernails scrawling codex
messages across the tissue paper skin
                              of my forearm.
I am becoming fluent in the language
                    of breathing,

Some days
I am afraid of the way
moonlight clings to the underside
oh her jawline when our hips
                glide together primordial
through the flushed streetlamp hush
of twilight.

Her smile carves canyons
into the clay of my
                    complexion.
I can't help but wonder at the notion
she doesn't realize how lovely she is.

I amy heavy geode heart bursting with purple.
I beg her two hands into sledgehammers,
realize a long drop isn't the only way to crack.
This doesn't feel like falling.

Display type set in Didot, Mona Lisa, Palatino, democratica & Sabon.

Georgia is used for punctuation in conjunction with Palatino texts, except when not; headings set in Palatino; epigraphs set in Didot, except when not.

Scissors Rock Paper bottlecaps, Sessions lager, Hood River, Or.

of first lines

index

After each war: / I counted my teeth ...   15
A group of hummingbirds is called a charm   81
a hicky / isn't technically a kiss / but i leave them on your skin ...   70
and / in the morning / the crows have turned ...   63
Be anything except indifferent towards me.   26
Because my father was a mountain my mother couldn't move   14
down by the bay / where lighthouses i have / never known rust   24
Even my silence knows your name   54
Every year with the predictability / of seasons   18
'fusbal / is not rugby'   29
Here is what I know: / whether you remove / a bandaid slowly...   18
"hot wonder, funny face. ..."   42
How long does it take / a letter to cover 176 miles ...   69
if i were a honeybee / i'd be a sting,   53
I am a fucked up / majestic little / universe   54
I am a known breaker of broken things   20
i asked the spine of a book ...   81
i don't know / the circumference / of the earth / or the ...   80
"i hope your skeletons / found somewhere else ..."   46
I'm sorry. / I killed the african violet ...   41
In last night's shot glass / mix equal parts regret and / don't-give-a-fuck   34
I told you I loved you / before I knew it was true.   43
i want to call you persephone.   67
i want you / to say my name / the way martyrs say / prayers: ...   57
I was the last person to see you alive: / bloodied nose in a dive bar ...   71
It is probaby foolish / (and more than a little vain) ...   47
I wrote a poem and called it / *The Color of Your Eyes*...   35
Kiss me like keys kiss locks.   42
last night i dreamed / my grandfather's bare chest ...   37
Last year you tried to teach me / how to choose the perfect avocado.   87
leave your skin / on the bedroom floor.   37
Let's set out before the / sun comes up / travel east or west until / we run
        out of east / or west   33
Meet me at / the unraveling —   25
My body is an empty den.   26
my co-worker / speaks / beaten dog / fluently ...   74

My father is Appalachia *noun*   58
On that couch in the yard, at the edge of adulthood, / you told me that
    falling is the laziest way to gain admiration.   88
raindrops and the sound of ghosts / have followed me around ...   73
Razor blades and india ink / on the bedside table   29
remember / four years old, arizona / sunlight baking the ...   76
Some days / I am afraid of the way / my skin begs for her affection   90
The city is / wearing / your eye color again   55
The house hunkers low   48
The night our friendship fell down the stairs   22
The summer we were fucked up kids / I replaced my fingerprints...   38
The year I graduated high school ...   68
There is a girl back home / who smells like powdered sugar.   64
there is a girl i've learned to kiss, / trapping her tongue between my teeth   77
This is not a story. / This is four days / of snow like a stifled scream ...   59
This morning / (I was buying an avocado / in a store where...   32
Today / I ate the first peach / since you died.   78
Today at a bus stop / a girl shared her umbrella with me   25
today / i want to be / a young johnny depp ...   75
Tuesday / The fault lines of your mother's breakdown begin to/ echo
    through your hollow bones,   50
with the history of tonight / splashed purple (like the voice of god)   81
when i asked you / to fuck me / i meant to say / there is shrapnel / in my
    lungs from   86
When I was a child there was/ a particular breed of movie scene, ...   62
When I was young / my mother measured / the length of   16
When the doctor asks / if I have allergies / I laugh and ...   74
When the miles / get caught in your throat: 56
when the monster / takes your knees ...   68
You and I / We never watched scary movies ...   47
You cast yourself into the desert / where there is no air / there you /
    wander   89
You tried to tell me purple was for hope —   30
You were a hometown: ...   42

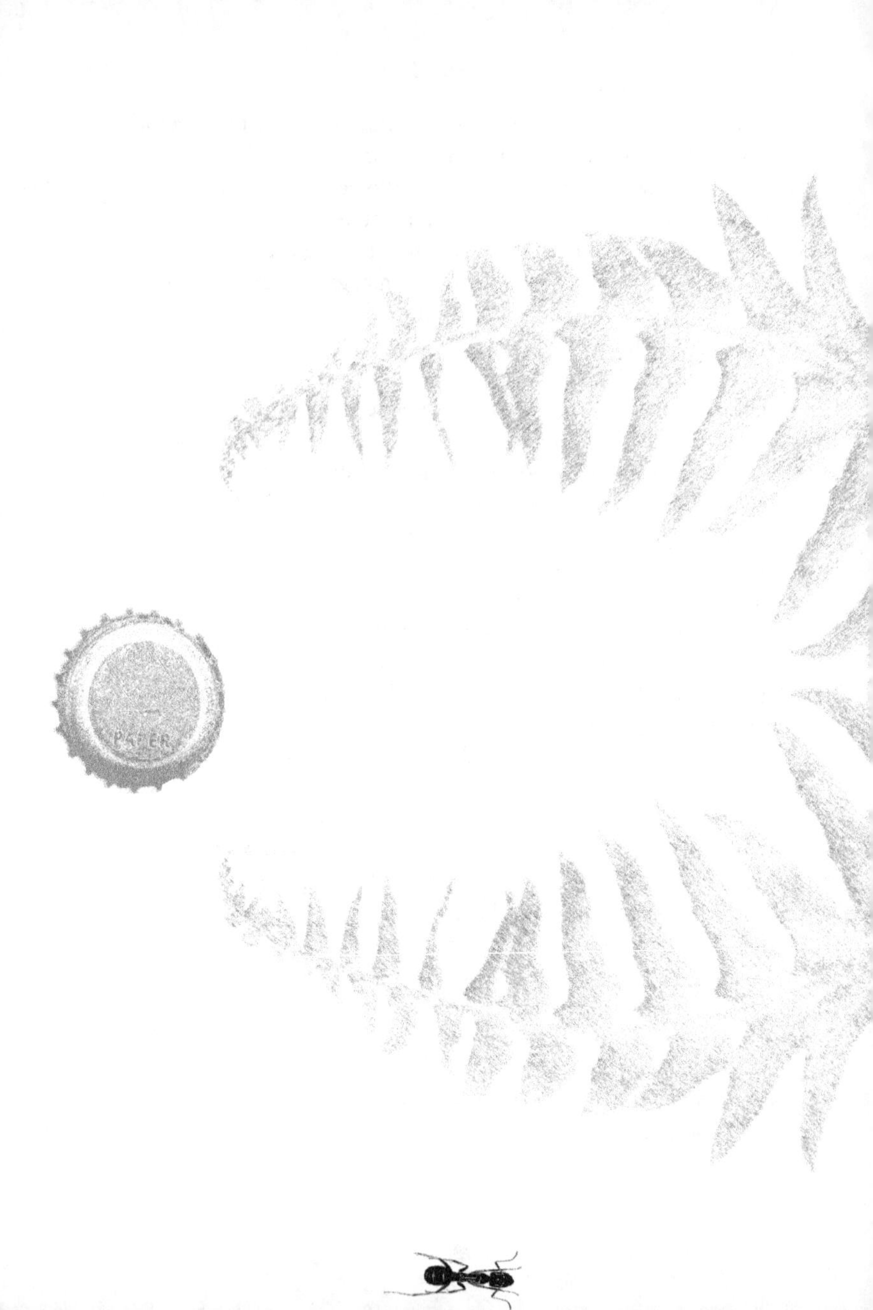

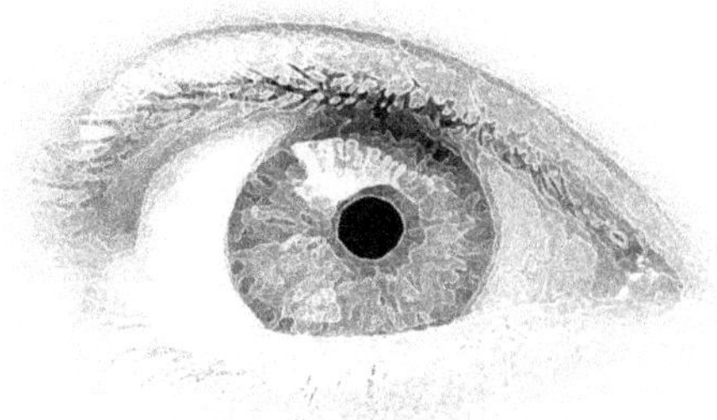

Brenda Taulbee, a Missoula, Montana transplant, came to Portland, Oregon in 2012 with aspirations of playing international rugby. Prior to moving she studied Anthropology & Linguistics at the University of Montana. Her variety of odd jobs include burrito-slinger, manager of a doggie daycare, & a very brief interlude as a roofer. To pump it up on her way to work she listens to Kimya Dawson, Regina Spektor, Ingrid Michaelson, etc. Unwinding her way home she defaults to her iTunes shuffle.

Brenda had her first public reading, Sept., 2012, through the Stone Soup Reading series in Portland & published her chapbook, *Dances with Bears...& Other Ways to Lose a Limb*, in June 2013. Her work has published in several literary print & online magazines & publications, incl. *Gobshite Quarterly* (completely multilingual en-face semi-annual flip book double trouble double issue), *The Inflectionist Review*, *The Los Angeles Review*, *Grist*, *Nailed*, & *UnderGround Books*. She has just completed an MFA writing program at SDSU, & returned to Portland, where she is working on her thesis with her cat, Murphy's Law.